ALSO BY BETTE MIDLER

A View from A Broad

The Saga of BABY DIVINE

by BETTE MIDLER

ILLUSTRATED BY TODD SCHORR

CROWN PUBLISHERS, INC., NEW YORK

Inquiries should be addressed to Crown Publishers, Inc., One Park Avenue, New York, New York 10016

Printed in the United States of America

Published simultaneously in Canada by General Publishing Company Limited

Library of Congress Cataloging in Publication Data
Midler, Bette.
  The saga of Baby Divine.
  I. Schorr, Todd.   II. Title.
PS3563.I365S3   1983   811'.54   83-7441
ISBN 0-517-55040-7

10 9 8 7 6 5 4 3 2 1

First Edition

For Fred

The Skies were ablaze with Disorder that Night,
The Planets, aghast and aquiver;
The Delirious Moon had the Brass to be Full
When it should have been only a sliver.

A Comet appeared, and those who dared peek
Say Stars fell to Earth in a Panic;
Historians claim that the Cosmos eclipsed
The Excesses of Darryl F. Zanuck!

Yes, Heaven had worked itself into a Frenzy
Of Wild and Transcendent Design
To herald the Glory of what was to come—
The Birth of Baby Divine!

Oh, Baby Divine, what an Entrance—
As Demure as the Fourth of July!
Mr. and Mrs. Divine didn't know
If they ought to Rejoice or to Cry.

Poor Dears! They had lived a Most Circumspect Life
In a house on a Nondescript Road,
Surrounded by houses exactly like theirs,
All with neat little lawns, neatly mowed.

And since nothing too Madcap or Garish or Wacky
Was ever allowed in that Quarter,
The Proper Divines had good reason to hope
For a Proper, Presentable Daughter.

So you can imagine their Terrible Shock
When they lay down their Babe in her bed
And found she'd arrived with High Heels on her feet
And a Sprig of Red Hair on her head.

But the Heels and the Hair-do were only the Prologue—
Another Great Shock lay in store,
For their Baby had already mastered a word
And the word she had mastered was "MORE!"

Yes, "MORE!" she crowed clearly, and yet again "MORE!"
The Elder Divines nearly fainted.
Then she followed that feat with a Luminous Smile
Much as Giotto himself might have painted.

But while the Divines stood there wringing their hands
There were cheers in another Location—
A Section of Town the Divines only knew
By its Scurrilous Reputation.

Where Baubles and Bangles and Silly *Ensembles*
Replaced Polyester and Chintz,
And no one would deem it *outré* if a Baby
Wore Heels or a Red Henna Rinse.

In fact, who would notice a Baby at all—
No matter how chubby her torso—
When day after day was like Mardi Gras Time,
And night after night even more so!

Here no one would snub you or look down their nose
If your Coat or your Mind were in tatters;
Be What You Want to Be, that was their creed,
It's the State of Your Spirit that Matters!

And smack in the midst of this Hullabaloo,
In a Boardinghouse close to the Track,
Snoozed Three Dizzy Dames whose room seemed to have
Undergone a Ferocious Attack:

Lily and Tillie and Joyce were their names,
And they lived in a Heap on the floor;
At lunch and at length they would gab about
        Art
And Theatrical Legend and Lore.

For Tillie had been (in the Days of her Youth)
Adored as a Terpsichorine.
She danced with Abandon and not too much
        else,
Yet never approached the Obscene.

And Lily sang Opera and Lieder and such
And was quite the Tempestuous Wench.
She sang with a Passion and Diction to match,
But lamentably only in French.

And Joyce? She told jokes that were top of the
        line—
Like the one about Midge and Godzilla.
Twenty-two people died laughing at that one—
The Punchline was really a Killer!

Well, as Legend goes, on the Night of the Birth,
Ribbons of Radiant Light
Awakened Miss Tillie, who ran to the Window
And squawked like a Duck at the Sight:

"Girls! Girls! Get up right away!
Come here! Look outside! Do you see?
The Sky over there by the House of Divine!
Is lit up like a Giant Marquee!"

Well, needless to say, at the sound of *that* word
The Ladies leapt up in a flash,
For it harkened them back to those Ballyhoo Days
When their act was a Certified Smash.

They pulled off their Jammies; they threw on their
    Pearls;
They powdered and rouged to excess;
They bumbled and fumbled and flew down the Street
Till they came to the Hallowed Address.

They stood on the Doorstep and gaped at the Sky.
A Shower of Sheet Music fell.
They shrieked: "What *is* going *on* around here?"
And nervously rang the Front Bell.

But no one came forward to pierce the Enchantment;
They felt they were lost in a Dream.
"I say," Lily whispered, "this *is* rather odd.
If they don't answer soon I shall scream!"

"Oh, calm down!" Joyce hissed. "Lily, calm down
    this instant.
Some restraint, for a change, would be nice.
Yes, restraint would be nice," Joyce said over again,
For she loved to say everything twice.

"Now cut it out, Ladies!" Miss Tillie chimed in.
"This isn't the time to be fighting.
Just look at this Sky! Why, I coulda been
A *Star* if *I*'d had this lighting!"

At last the Divines opened up the Front Door.
"We gave at the Office," they said.
But the overwrought trio paid no heed at all
For they'd spotted the Babe in her bed.

"Brava! Oh, Brava!" they squealed at the Child
As they elbowed her Parents aside
In their hurry to hug her and swoon at her feet—
The Starchy Divines nearly died!

"Just look at those Fabulous Shoes!" Tillie
    shouted.
"I wish I could get me a pair!
And who could resist that ridiculous Smile
Or the Color and Curl of that Hair!"

Then Tillie untangled her Favorite Boa—
More precious than Diamonds or Furs—
And said: "I got this from an Ardent Marquis,
But now she must have it. It's hers!"

And Joyce offered up a decrepit false nose
Which she swore was bequeathed by the Czar.
"It's a prop for those times when you want to
    become
Someone else, someone else than you are."

And Lil said: "My gift may seem less than
    expected,
But, my dear, it's far more than it seems."
And proudly she pulled from the depths of her
    handbag
A Flutter of Rainbow and Dreams.

Baby Divine was quite giddy with Joy;
She felt her young heart start to soar.
She wanted to sing: "Oh, you've made me so
    Happy!"
But all she could manage was "MORE!"

"I'm sorry! How *awful*!" cried Mrs. Divine.
"My own flesh and blood so ungrateful!"
"Oh, pipe down!" said Tillie. "Be proud that she's
    talking.
It's really more funny than hateful."

"So true," nodded Lil. "Why, it's actually
    charming
And good for the kid to want more.
Total contentment is only for cows.
It tends to turn tots into bores."

"STOP IT! GET OUT!" bellowed Mr. Divine,
"This Baby is batty enough!
The last thing we need is to have her head
    filled
With all that Bohemian stuff!"

"Well!" sniffed the three, stomping out in a huff
And muttering much as they went,
"These people are Fools! Can't they see that the kid
Has undoubtedly been Heaven-sent?"

Now the Baby, of course, didn't *mean* to say "MORE!"
She meant "Thanks!" (which is far more polite).
She was feeling despondent and misunderstood
When suddenly out went the light.

Baby Divine didn't care for the Dark;
Still, she wasn't exactly afraid,
For in the next room were her Ma and her Pa
And the Sleepytime Noises they made.

"That's *my* pillow, dear!" and "Move *over,* please!"
Were some of the sounds that she heard.
But then the poor baby heard something so frightful
She wished that she'd not heard a word.

"That Baby's not ours!" her Father exclaimed.
"Those Shoes! And that Hair! She's a Quack!
I'm positive somebody made a mistake.
Should we think about giving her back?"

"Oh, dear," sighed her Mother, "I know what
      you mean.
If only she weren't so flashy!
I know this is odd for a Mother to say—
But I find her—well—just a bit trashy!"

The Baby recoiled as if someone had slapped her.
This Censure was so unexpected!
Was she really so worthless? Really so strange?
Why was she being rejected?

To whom could she turn? From whom could she learn
What it takes in this Life to belong?
Those Ladies who gave her the Presents, of course!
They could tell her at once what was wrong.

But where were they now? And what did it matter?
She was, after all, just a Tyke.
She never could reach them. From where she was lying
The Front Door alone was a Hike.

It would take her forever to crawl on all fours
But the Child, ever hopeful, thought maybe
If she tried very hard she could walk like a grown-up
And not have to creep like a baby.

She pulled herself up to the edge of her cradle
And tossed herself out on that chance.
She found out at once she could not walk a step
But, whoopee, could she ever dance!

She whirled and she twirled on the tips of her toes!
She unveiled an Exquisite *Plié*.
She crashed through the door with a Wild *Pirouette*
And eagerly went on her way.

But she got only one *entrechat* out the door
When she suddenly stopped on a dime.
And her heart skipped a beat as, gasping, she gazed
On the World for the very first time.

Trees under Starlight; Meadows in Mist;
Houses and Fences and Sky—
When the Moon sallied forth from behind a Black
        Cloud
Why, Baby Divine thought she'd die!

And there in the Moonlight she glimpsed a White Rose
Her Mother had planted in Spring;
Her kneecaps grew weak with the Beauty of it,
And Her Broken Heart started to sing.

"MORE! MORE!" she shrieked and she shried,
And almost as if the World heard
A Sycamore rustled, and out of the tree
Flew a rather Preposterous Bird.

Holy Toledo! thought Baby Divine,
Whoever conceived of such things?
A creature that's able to fly through the air!
What a thrill it must be to have Wings!

And then, just as though the Bird read Baby's mind
He lightly touched down on her Shoulder.
"You're right. It's a thrill! Come and see for yourself.
You can trust me," the scruffy Bird told her.

" 'Cause I've been around. I've been up. I've been
          down.
I look and I listen. I learn.
It's a tricky old Globe, kid—and I oughta know,
'Cause I'm not just some dim-witted tern.

"And I bet that a Baby with Heels and Red Hair
Will probably think it's terrific.
You'll squeal with delight as we go for the Sun
And applaud when we hit the Pacific!"

Well, not on your life would our Baby Divine
Say no to a chance to go soaring.
She clambered right up on the little Bird's back—
She was really quite mad for Exploring.

Off they both sailed toward a Dinner-plate Moon,
Over Highways and Houses and Trees.
They soared with panache through a Cloud made of Silk
And a Bumbling of Vagabond Bees.

But while Baby Divine and the Bird were in Heaven,
Her Parents were down in the dumps,
For they'd found to their Horror their Offspring
     was missing,
And, Brother, did they feel like chumps!

It was Mrs. Divine who discovered the fact
That her little Tot's Cradle was bare;
She'd gone in to change both the Babe and her Bottle
And only the Bottle was there.

How pale with Foreboding she flew to the Door,
Crying out to her spouse, "There's a track!
The Footsteps are teensy and murder to follow
But darling, we *must* fetch her back!"

The Anxious Divines grabbed their coats and their
        flashlights
And started to follow the trail,
But twenty yards into the Garden it stopped—
Their Girlhunt seemed destined to fail.

Was she snatched off the Earth? Was she deep in a hole?
Was she kidnapped? Oh, no, God Forbid!
Who'd kidnap *that* Screwball? Of course! It's those Dames!
They sure were gung ho for the kid.

"Let's find them," cried Mrs. Divine, "and confront them!
I know we can ferret them out!"
And off they both ran, while a Mile Overhead
The Babe and the Bird soared about.

Curving round Moonbeams, they dipped with the
        Breeze—
Higher, still higher, they flew.
The Baby was stunned when she glanced toward the
        Earth
And beheld the Spectacular View!

But it wasn't the Beauty alone that amazed her—
Though that in itself was to die—
What caused her Red Hair to uncurl was how odd
Her neighborhood looked from the sky.

For everything that she had thought was So Big
Looked terribly Puny and Small
And what had seemed Hugely Important close up
Seemed not that important at all.

For instance, her house—which had seemed so Enormo—
Was hardly *Tyrannosaur Rex,*
And the town she called Home—just a glimmer of
    Lights
In the shape of a Capital *X*!

Of course, Baby D, being smart as a whip,
Did not feel confused, but instead,
Felt the Glorious Thrill she would feel every time
A Great Truth penetrated her head.

THE TRUTH
It's the Point of Your View that Decides What You See—
One Man's Flop Is Another Man's Hit.
From Manners to Movies, the Picture Keeps Changing
Depending Upon Where You Sit.

But still there was more for the Babe to absorb
As they zigzagged their way through the Sky.
A Further Surprise was that even the *Mountains*
All looked just *alike* from on high.

And she thought why if it's such a job for a *Mountain*
To stand out from all of the rest
How hard it must be for a minuscule *Human*!
And suddenly Baby felt blessed!

My Shoes! My Red Hair! They're my Trump cards! she thought.
Then her Brain formed this Pithy Bon Mot:
Cherish Forever What Makes You Unique
Cause You're Really a Yawn If It Goes!

The Babe felt like Einstein, like Kant, like Descartes
As she pondered this New Revelation—
To the Wonders and Whimsical Ways of the World
Her Soul gave a Standing Ovation!

Now just at that Moment the Elder Divines
Arrived at the Ladies' Front Door.
They barged right on in and tripped over Lil,
Who was out like a light on the floor.

They yelled in the Darkness, "Oh, give us our
    Baby!"
The Ladies awoke to a scare,
As the Frantic Divines fairly ransacked their
    room
In search of some Shining Red Hair.

"How dare you accuse us!" The Dames were aghast.
"This insult is too much to take!"
One look at their faces convinced the Divines
They had made an Appalling Mistake.

"We're friends!" Tillie cried. "You should ask
    for our help,
Which of course we'd be tickled to grant."
"You take the High Road and we'll take the Low
    Road,"
Lil trilled in a Dainty Descant.

Her voice was so piercing the Babe could have
    heard,
But a Thunderstorm rose from the Sea.
Though the Bird and the Babe did their best to
    avoid it,
The Tempest would not let them be.

It smacked them and wracked them and blew them
    around
Till they shook like a Crepe-paper Ship.
Then one blast of Thunder and—Horror of Horrors!—
Baby Divine lost her grip!

Head over diaper, she fell toward the Earth,
So swiftly she heard the Wind whine.
She clasped her small hands and looked toward
    the Heavens
And prayed she was *truly* Divine!

And as Fate would have it, her Shoes saved the day,
For though she came down like a rock,
Her Heels were designed by Monsieur Charles Jourdan,
So, of course, they absorbed all the shock.

But though she survived, she was still in a pickle,
Alone, and so far from her home.
If only somebody would come by to help her
And lend her a Map or a Comb.

Ever Brave and Resourceful, the Baby thought: Wait!
I really must try and calm down.
I'll just stretch out my arms and flap-flap like the Bird
Till I flap myself right off the ground!

Then in her Mind's Eye she saw herself clearly
Falling again from the Sky.
Ka-boom went her Heart; her legs turned to Jelly;
Her mouth tasted tinny and dry.

"YOU'LL NEVER FLY!" boomed a Voice from the
      Dark,
And terror struck Baby Divine
As a Figure in Black lumbered toward her and
      thundered:
"At last, Little Lady, you're mine!"

The Figure was Fearful and Dismal and Huge
And wrapped in a Sulfurous Fog.
It had snakes round its ankles and moss round its
      heart
And its voice was as hoarse as a Frog's.

Even the Moon was afraid of its Presence
And hurriedly slipped out of sight.
The Air grew Chilly and Sickly and Damp
And a Tremor of Dread shook the Night.

"I am Anxiety, friend to Despair!
I appear when your Courage departs.
I find you whenever your Confidence fails you
And Fear makes a Home in your Heart!"

Well, Baby Divine didn't like this at all.
In fact, she was frightened to death.
She started to dance away fast as she could,
But the poor thing was soon out of breath.

"Go on!" cried Anxiety. *"Dance for your Life!*
This isn't the last time we'll meet.
You'd better learn now there's no way to escape me,
For I'm very fast on my feet!"

To show her the Terrible Truth in his words,
The Figure, Colossal and Dank,
Charged through the night after Baby Divine,
And as it pursued her, it stank!

It stank and galobbled and belched as it lurched
Toward the Baby who fell in a swoon,
And as it came nearer its Eyes caught on Fire
And Midnight lit up like High Noon.

Then, oh, in a moment too creepy to mention,
The Fiend bent down with a grunt;
He picked up the Child by the scruff of her neck
And said, *"Say Your Bye-byes, you Runt!"*

He swung her way out like a Doll on a String;
From his throat came a deafening Roar.
But all the poor Baby could do was to scream
For the last thing she wanted—"MORE!"

"MORE! MORE!" she pathetically piped,
And instantly she became very
Aware of the dangers inherent in having
A limited Vocabulary.

Well, I've had it now, the Besieged Baby thought
As she whizzed past those Eyeballs in Flames—
When suddenly who should sprint onto the
     Scene
But those Three Irrepressible Dames.

Anxiety reared up and howled when he
     saw them.
Undaunted, Lil cried: "Fiddlesticks!
Just look at this Big Bag of Wind! What a Humbug!
Let's hit him with *our* Bag of Tricks!"

Lil opened the onslaught by screeching Off-key;
Joyce battered the Thing with some Schtick.
Crying, *"En garde!"* Tillie finished him off
With a rather unladylike kick.

"Whew, that was close!" said Miss Tillie to Joyce.
"It's a good thing we tracked the kid down."
Baby Divine *arabesqued* in relief
And they laughed till they fell on the ground.

And Anxiety, lurking in shadows nearby,
Fled in a Mad Disarray,
For a good, hearty laugh was a Threat to his Health
And certain to drive him away.

The Baby was bug-eyed. Where did the Fiend come from?
She sensed a Divine Revelation.
The Beast had been born of her very own Fears—
The Monster was her own Creation!

"You Imp! Why, you Imp!" cried a breathless Miss
    Joyce.
"You put us through torture!" cried Lily.
"Now, girls," Tillie said, "grab ahold of yourselves.
To be mad at an Infant is silly.

"Just think of the problems this kid's had to face.
She's as mixed up as Lily's Chop Suey.
She's got to be taught what's Important and what
Is only a Crockful of Hooey."

And Lil said: "Then laughter's the place to begin.
It keeps life from being a bore.
With a good sense of humor, she'll always be rich;
Without one, she'll always be poor."

Baby Divine sat and played with her Step-ins;
Joyce murmured, "But where shall we start?
Laughter, like Life, comes in *all* shapes and sizes.
She must learn to tell them apart."

"Let's start with the *giggle*," said Lil, "it's the
    smallest
And rather undignified, too.
Giggles and titters are laughs that slip out
Whenever a laugh is taboo.

"Next there's the *chuckle,* a satisfied laugh,
A cluck to yourself that feels good."
Baby Divine fluffed some hairs on her head
And chuckled, 'cause she understood.

"But then there's the mean and insensitive
      snicker,
Disrespectful and low on civility.
It's a bit *un peu trop* for a child of your taste
And highly refined sensibility."

Poor Baby Divine had to race to keep up—
She'd not heard these distinctions before;
She wanted to scream, "I have had quite enough,"
But out came her usual: "MORE!"

"Well, all right," said Tillie, "let's end with
      the loudest,
The mighty and rowdy *guffaw.*
When you are guffawing, you're laughing so hard
You may end up flat on the floor!"

Well, Baby Divine thought guffaws sounded great,
Raucous and Free and Sublime.
She threw back her head, she doubled in half,
And laughed for the very first time.

And, oh, it felt good just to laugh and to laugh—
Such a whoopingly nice thing to do.
She thought, I must do this a lot in my life
And make sure that others do too.

Then Joyce said, "Now child, now child, that's
    enough.
Not all things in Life are so droll.
A good laugh is good for the spirits, it's true,
But a good *cry* is good for the soul."

And with that the Ladies began to boohoo,
And to weep and to wail and to moan.
And teardrops welled up in their eyes like the
    Sea,
And many a nose was blown.

But Baby Divine simply hadn't a clue
As to what they were doing or why.
Said Lily, "That's simply a brief demonstration
Of the sad little verb—*to cry*.

"However," cried Lily, "let's not dwell on *that*!
The Child has absorbed quite a lot.
And crying is something she'll learn by her lonesome
Whether she wants to or not.

"So stop with the Lessons. Let's give her a Treat!
The show that once made us all Famous!"
What's a *show*? thought the Babe, and she hoped against
    Hope
That she wasn't a Short Ignoramus.

"But we did so many!" whined Tillie, perplexed.
"Which one do you think would most please her?
The Pageant? The Farce? The Mystery Play?
Or the Ear scene from *Julius Caesar*?

"Something with Music, of course!" cried Miss Tillie.
"We want to show off all our stuff!
There'll be Kick lines and Punch lines and Ditties and
    Damnèd
Be he who first cries: 'Hold enough!'

"There's no time to dally. Let's put it in gear!"
And they flew like Giselles on their way.
Baby Divine did her best to keep up
With a perfectly swell *grand jeté*.

They came to a halt in a Darkened Backyard
Where some Laundry was hung on a line.
And they vowed as they pulled off the things that they
    needed,
"We'll have them back here in no time!"

Til wrapped round her tummy a colorful sheet
As they do in some Russian resorts,
While Joyce tried to fashion the *Folies-Bergere*
From an Elderly Gentleman's shorts.

Lily encircled her head many times
In a Towel that still was quite damp.
On top of this Turban she slapped some Red Cherries
And bellowed: "Now, Ladies, let's vamp!

"For it *is* nearly midnight. Our Costumes are done,
And each is a Stellar Creation!
It's truly amazing what you can pull off
If you use your Imagination."

Oh, no! What's *that*? the Babe wondered, confused.
Then Lil said, "Add this to your list:
Your imagination's the talent to think
Of things that don't really exist."

"Now all that we need," Tillie furrowed her brow,
"Are some lights and a stage and a curtain."
"Why, Tillie," chirped Lily, "just open your eyes.
We've plenty to work with, that's certain.

"That tree stump will serve as a marvelous stage,
The Moon will provide us with Light.
And what better curtain than that lovely willow?"
The Baby could tell Lil was right.

"Now, places!" Lil shouted. "The show must
    go on!"
And, oh, from the very first cue,
The Act was a Clutter of Thrilling Delights—
There was nothing those Gals couldn't do.

Lil sang an Air about Thugs in Montmartre
And the contraband truffles they sold.
Her hair stood on end as she hit the last note
And a poodle nearby passed out cold.

And Joyce came onstage as a Pizza to Go.
There never was anyone like her;
Her jokes were so funny that Baby Divine
Thought that someone had best change her
    diaper.

Tillie performed a short Tango to start,
Then offered a Sparkling Gavotte
Which segued right into a One-footed Hula
That had them all glued to the spot.

"MORE! MORE!" cried Baby Divine.
(She'd never seen grown-ups so jolly!)
Then she noticed that Lily was calling for her
To join in the Gala Finale.

That's all that it took! She jumped to her feet!
Her Soul heard the Call of the Stage.
She was running full tilt toward the Lights and the
     Magic
When a Voice bellowed out in a Rage:

"You on the Stage? What astonishing gall!
You're a Nothing! A Washout! A Nerd!
You think you're so cute and so charming? Well, kid,
You're not only dumb—you're Absurd!"

Yes, there was Anxiety! Right on the stage!
As ugly and heartless as ever!
"What's stopping you, Sweetheart? Lost all your
     nerve?
Well, guess when you'll find it? NEVER!"

Now the Ladies were quite unaware of the Brute;
They continued their warbling and wiggling
Right in the Face of the Furious Fiend—
And suddenly Baby was giggling!

That's right, Baby giggled! And then she guffawed—
Which the Monster could just not believe.
The stronger her laughter, the weaker he grew,
Till he sheepishly squeaked: *"Think I'll leave."*

He practically tripped over Tillie's pink sheet
In his hurry to exit Stage Right;
He shrank like a Sweater till all that was left
Was a Grimace of Rage in the Night.

And then it was over. The Terror was gone.
Baby flew onto the Stage.
Some Primeval Instinct propelled her Down
      Center—
And Theatrical Art came of age!

She basked in the Limelight and knew she had found
A place where she'd always belong.
Her Spirit took flight and she did what she could
To join in this Jubilant Song:

More

C   **C#°**

1. So you've been to the alps,— and you've been to the Bal - tic, you've
Lat - in is per - fect, you've mem-o-rized Shake-speare, you

Dm   **G7**   **Dm**   **G7**

swat-ted your way— thru Pe - ru.   You've seen ev-'ry is - land you
know how to add— two and two.   You've learned ev-'ry-thing— that you

Dm   **G7**   **C**   **C7**

want-ed to see— when an old friend drops out of the blue, say-in,'
want-ed to know— when a wise man on his way to Kat-man-du, says,

F   **Fm**   **C/E**   **C/D**   **C**

"I got us seats on a rock-et to Mars, it's like noth-ing you ev-er saw— be-
"I'd like to teach you the mean-ing of life, hard-ly an-y-one — knows it — any-

A   **A7**   **Dm7**   **G**

fore!"   Do you say, "I've seen e-nough!"   No!_____   You want to see ⎱
more."   Do you say, "I know e-nough!"   No!_____   You want to know ⎰

C   **Am**

More, more, more, more, more, more, more,— more, more, more, more, more,—

Dm

More, more, more, more, more, more, more,— more, more, more, more, more!—

1. G7   **2. G7**   **Ab**

2. So your ___   Then he says,   "When_____ it comes to

And as the Spectacular drew to its close
Who should come out of the Woods
But the Elder Divines who watched openmouthed
As their Baby delivered the Goods!

They heard her sing note after note like Tebaldi,
They saw her *chassé* like Pavlova.
The Staggering Passion she brought to her Act
Was something they couldn't get over!

How foolish they felt! How Stupidly Stuffy!
They'd been too myopic to see
Their Child was a Treasure, a Gem to be cherished—
A Baby *Divine,* indeed.

Mr. and Mrs. Divine were Ecstatic!
They whistled, they stomped, and they cheered.
When they called to their Baby, "We love you! We
      love you!"
The Babe shed her Very First Tear.

Finally, all of the bows were completed;
The Ebullient Mrs. Divine
Rushed up to her child, throwing flowers and kisses,
Crying, "Oh, I'm so *glad* you are mine!"

"Now wait," said Miss Tillie, "I must ask the kid
If she thought we were good or a bore."
But the only response out of Baby Divine—
Of course you have guessed it—was "MORE!"

"Oh, no!" laughed Miss Joyce with a sigh of relief,
"No more. Please, no more for tonight.
In a very few moments the Sun will be up
And we're not at our best in the Light."

"So come, Everyone, the Festivity's over.
It's time we all headed back home.
There are limits to everything—even to Fun—
Remember what happened to Rome."

And off went the Troupe, a most Fetching Sextet,
All happily prancing away.
Her Mom and her Dad beamed as Baby kept up
With a turbulent *pas de bourrée*.

They were all out of breath when they reached the
    Divines'
(The Baby had tripped once or twice);
And there at the Doorway the Ladies bent down
And panted this Prudent Advice:

"Make sure that your Life is a Rare Entertainment!
It doesn't take anything drastic.
You needn't be gorgeous or wealthy or smart
Just Very Enthusiastic!"

The Baby looked up with great Love in her heart,
Quite moved by her friends' Valediction,
And Farewells took place such as one only finds
In later Victorian fiction.

The Ladies soon vanished like Stars in the Morning,
For Daylight was quickly advancing.
The Elder Divines said, "It's been quite a night,
    Dear;
It's sleep you need now, not more dancing."

Baby Divine *Saut de Basqued* through the Door,
And into her cradle she leapt.
Her eyes were half-closed; she was pooped as
     can be,
But *so* glad that she hadn't slept!

For she'd learned how to Laugh, and she'd learned
     how to Cry
And to use her Imagination.
The loss of some sleep seemed a small price to pay
For *such* a Divine Education!

And just to make everything even more rosy,
Her folks said, "We know we were rude,
But won't your forgive us? We love you like crazy."
Then they kissed her and tenderly cooed:

Lullabye

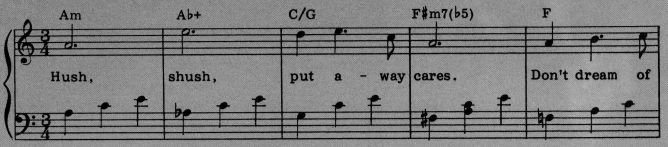

Hush,   shush,   put a - way cares.   Don't dream of

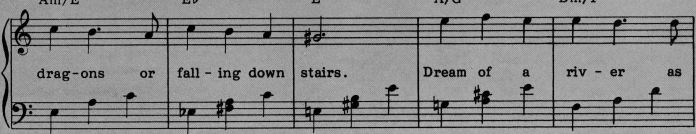

drag-ons   or   fall - ing down stairs.   Dream of a   riv - er   as

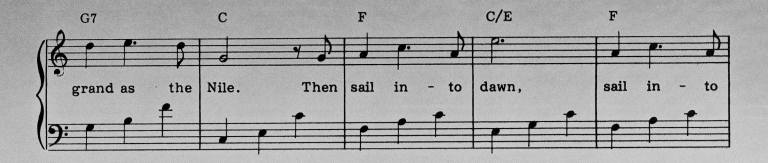

grand as   the   Nile.   Then sail in - to dawn,   sail in - to

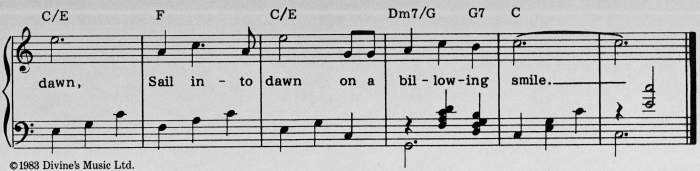

dawn,   Sail in - to dawn   on a bil - low-ing   smile.

Then they tucked in her Boa, they smoothed her Red Hair;
Then the Elder Divines went to bed.
Baby Divine was alone in the Dark
But it no longer filled her with dread.

For she thought of her folks and the Dames and
        their Gifts—
The Garland, the Boa, the Nose—
And she thought of the Bird that had taken her
        soaring,
And she thought of her Mother's White Rose.

And Baby Divine felt the Call and the Challenge
Of Life and the Urge to Explore,
And she vowed as she started to dream of
        Tomorrow
To never stop calling for "MORE!"

A Note about the Type

The text of this book was set on Mergenthaler 202 equipment in a face called Cheltenham Bold, originally designed as a linotype face by the architect Bertram Grosvenor Goodhue, in collaboration with Ingalls Kimball of the Cheltenham Press of New York.

Cheltenham was introduced in the early twentieth century, a period of remarkable achievement in type design. The idea of creating a "family" of types by making variations on the basic type design was originated by Goodhue and Kimball in the design of the Cheltenham series.